BAD GUYS

PIRATES

BAD GUYS

PIRATES

by Gary L. Blackwood

BENCHMARK BOOKS

MARSHALL CAVENDISH
NEW YORK

Benchmark Books
Marshall Cavendish Corporation
99 White Plains Road
Tarrytown, New York 10591-9001
Website: www.marshallcavendish.com

Library of Congress Cataloging-in-Publication Data

Blackwood, Gary L.
Pirates / by Gary L. Blackwood
p.cm.—(Bad guys ; 5)
Includes bibliographical references (p.) and index.
Summary: Discusses notable pirates and their activities over four centuries, from Africa to the Caribbean.
ISBN 0-7614-1019-8 (lib. bdg.)
1. Pirates—Juvenile literature. [1. Pirates.] I. Title.

G535 .B56 2001   346.16'4—dc21   99-086674

Book Design by Gysela Pacheco

Picture research by Linda Sykes Picture Research, Hilton Head SC

Front cover, pages 54, 57: Stock Montage; pages 1, 37, 41, 42: © Corbis; page 7: Royal Geographical Society, London/ The Bridgeman Art Library; page 9: Howard Pyle's Book of Pirates; pages 12, 51: Culver Pictures; pages 14, 27: John Carter Brown Library at Brown University; pages 16, 48: Delaware Art Museum; pages 3-4, 20, 30: Corbis-Bettmann; pages 23, 55: Mary Evans Picture Library, London; page 32: North Wind Pictures; page 34: Colonial Williamsburg; pages 43, 44: New York Public Library; page 46: National Maritime Museum Picture Library; page 59: AKG London; page 61: PrivateCollection/ The Bridgeman Art Library

Printed in Italy

1 3 5 6 4 2

Contents

———

Introduction

For as long as merchant ships filled with trade goods and treasure have been sailing the seas, other ships manned by marauders have been preying on them.

Phoenician vessels plying the Mediterranean Sea in the sixth century B.C. were regularly attacked by pirates. By 330 B.C piracy was such a threat that Alexander the Great made a concerted—and unsuccessful—effort to stamp it out.

In 78 B.C. the future emperor of Rome, Julius Caesar, was captured and held for ransom by pirates from Cilicia—now part of Turkey. Caesar behaved more like a tyrant than a prisoner: he played dice with his captors; he demanded silence at night so he could sleep; he insisted on reading his poetry to the pirates and threatened to have them killed if they didn't praise it. After Caesar's release, he promptly returned with several ships full of armed men, who captured the Cilicians, cut their throats, and crucified them.

Trading vessels loaded down with spices and silks from the East were attacked so often that the second-century Greek geographer Ptolemy referred to the west coast of India as the "Pirate Coast." In 1290 Marco Polo wrote of whole fleets of pirate ships prowling the Indian coast.

Though pirates have plied their trade in every corner of the seven seas, our popular image of them comes from the rogues who plundered Spanish treasure ships in the Caribbean.

When Spain began to exploit the resources of the New World, it created new opportunities for pirates. In the late 1600s and early 1700s, the Caribbean Sea experienced what historian Frank Sherry calls "the most intense outbreak of seaborne banditry ever recored." The era is often labeled the Golden Age of piracy.

Spain considered Central America and the West Indies its exclusive territory; in fact the area was known as the Spanish Main. But as hard as they tried, the Spanish couldn't keep the New World to themselves.

As early as the 1530s, France, England, Portugal, and the Netherlands had been establishing small colonies in the Caribbean, especially on the island of Hispaniola. The colonists were mainly misfits of various sorts: religious and political refugees, criminals, exiles, deserters, runaway slaves, and indentured servants.

They survived by hunting wild pigs and cattle. From the local Arawak Indians they learned the art of smoking meat over a fire on a grating of green sticks called a *boucan*. The colonists themselves became known as *boucaniers*, or buccaneers.

At first the *boucaniers* merely traded with passing ships, exchanging smoked meat, hides, and tallow for guns, clothing, and rum. But when the Spanish tried to force the foreigners out, the *boucaniers* retaliated by attacking Spanish ships—and discovered a far easier way of making a living.

By 1640 they had banded together in a confederacy they called *les gens de la côte*, or the Brotherhood of the Coast. It was a very democratic organization. Before each expedition the *boucaniers* got together to plan strategy, elect officers, and sign an agreement called a *chasse-partie* that dictated how they would divide up any booty they seized.

In the early years of the Brotherhood, its members attacked mainly small vessels and rarely ventured far from their home bases on Hispaniola or Tortuga. But around 1665 a *boucanier* called Pierre Le Grand made a more daring raid. With twenty-eight followers he boarded a huge ship commanded by a Spanish vice admiral.

Pirate vessels often carried a crew of one or two hundred men, making it hard for any one pirate's share to be very great. But if the pirates seized a rich enough prize, each man's share could range from £1,000 to £4,000—an income equal to that of many great lords.

To motivate his men, Le Grand had a hole bored in the hull of his own boat, so there could be no retreat. The attack took the Spaniards completely by surprise. "Jesus bless us!" they cried. "Are these devils, or what are they?"

Eventually the Brotherhood of the Coast so dominated the Caribbean that Spain was forced to suspend most of its shipping. When Spain's dispute with England and France over the New World turned into open warfare, many *boucaniers* allied themselves with French and English privateers, the better to harass the Spanish.

These privateers were little better than pirates. One British admiral complained that "the conduct of all privateers is . . . so near piracy that I only wonder any civilized nation can allow them." The privateers did carry documents called "letters of marque and reprisal" that authorized them to prey on a specific enemy. They were expected to obey certain rules of conduct—and to hand over to their goverments a percentage of the loot they seized.

The *boucaniers* had no such authority and were bound by no such rules. They attacked ships of any nation, kept all the plunder for themselves, and treated prisoners however they chose.

Some *boucaniers* were relatively humane, putting captured crews ashore in a safe place, or even giving them a ship to sail home. Others, such as the pirate leader known as L'Olonnois, were merciless.

One

The Bloodthirsty Buccaneer

François L'Olonnois (or L'Olonnais) was one of the most resourceful and successful of the *boucaniers*. He was also, without a doubt, the most barbaric and bloodthirsty—literally. Legend has it that, each time he delivered a mortal blow with his cutlass, he licked the victim's blood from the blade.

He was born Jean-David Nau. His alias of L'Olonnois came from the name of his hometown, Les Sables d'Olone, on the west coast of France. In 1640, two hundred French boys had been taken against their will to the West Indies, where they were sold to plantation owners as indentured servants. Jean-David was probably too young to have been part of that group. But sometime within the next decade he, too, was kidnapped and forced into servitude on the island of Dominica.

When he had served out his time, Jean-David headed for Hispaniola, headquarters of the Brotherhood of the Coast. He became a sailor, and displayed such courage against the Spanish that the deputy governor of the nearby island of Tortuga gave him a ship of his own. L'Olonnois quickly earned a reputation, both for the rich cargoes he seized and for his ruthless treatment of prisoners.

Despite his reputation for ruthlessness, L'Olonnois had no trouble attracting followers, because he also had a reputation for being lucky and successful.

Around 1662 L'Olonnois had an experience that left him with a fierce hatred of the Spanish. His ship was wrecked in a storm off Campeche, in present-day Mexico. The crew got ashore safely, only to encounter a troop of Spanish soldiers. L'Olonnois was only wounded in the battle that ensued, but nearly all of his men were killed.

Alexander Exquemelin, a former *boucanier*, wrote an account of how L'Olonnois "took several handfuls of sand and mingled them with the blood of his own wounds, with which he besmeared his face and other parts of his body. Then hiding himself dextrously among the dead, he continued there until the Spaniards had quitted the field."

Once his wounds healed, L'Olonnois stole a canoe and made his way to Tortuga, where he obtained another ship and continued his criminal career. The governor of Cuba, dismayed to learn that L'Olonnois still lived, sent a warship after him. Instead of fleeing, L'Olonnois and his followers seized several fishing boats and, disguised as fishermen, boarded the Spanish ship. Taken by surprise, the Spaniards surrendered, only to have their heads lopped off. The pirates spared one man, who carried this message to the governor:

> *I shall never henceforward give quarter* [mercy] *to any Spaniard whatsoever; and I have great hopes I shall execute on your own person the very same punishment I have done upon them you sent against me.*

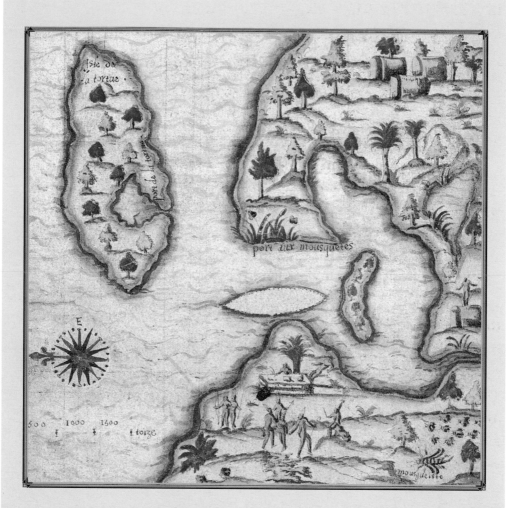

Labeled on this 1600 map as Isle de la tortue (Island of the Turtle), Tortuga was an ideal headquarters for pirate activity. In order to take advantage of the prevailing winds—known as trade winds—Spanish treasure ships had to sail right past the island.

As promised, L'Olonnois's tactics became even more ruthless. Not content with seizing the occasional ship, he resolved to hit the Spanish where they lived. His first target was Maracaibo, on the coast of Venezuela. In 1667 he arrived there with a fleet of eight ships and some six hundred fellow *boucaniers*. Exquemelin writes that, if any townsfolk refused to give up their money and valuables, L'Olonnois "would instantly cut them in pieces with his hanger (sword), and pull out their tongues; desiring to do the same, if possible, to every Spaniard in the world." Later, when a captured Spanish soldier angered him, he cut out the man's heart and gnawed on it "like a ravenous wolf."

As long as L'Olonnois managed to find rich plunder, his men overlooked his increasingly bizarre behavior. But when one prize—as captured ships were called—yielded nothing more valuable than bars of iron and jars of wine, most of the crew deserted him and went off, as the pirates put it, "on their own account."

Soon afterward L'Olonnois's ship ran aground. He and half his men set off in a small boat to seek help. But when they went ashore in what is now Panama, they were attacked by the local Indians, who proved even more merciless than L'Olonnois himself. They tore the living bodies of the captain and his companions into pieces, burned the pieces in a fire, and tossed the ashes to the winds.

Only one of the *boucaniers* escaped to tell Exquemelin the "history of the life and miserable death of that infernal wretch L'Ollonais, who, full of horrid, execrable and enormous deeds . . . died by cruel and butcherly hands, such as his own were in the course of his life."

The boucaniers *didn't prey exclusively on ships. The more audacious captains, such as L'Olonnois and Sir Henry Morgan, plundered whole cities. This painting dramatizes the 1697 sack of Cartagena, a port in what is now Colombia.*

Two

The Arch-Pirate

Near the end of the seventeenth century several things conspired to bring about the downfall of the Caribbean *boucaniers.* In 1688 England's King James offered a general pardon, which many of the pirates accepted. Some returned to Europe; others became traders and plantation owners.

The following year the *boucaniers* lost an ally when England made peace with Spain. The combined forces of England and Spain made piracy in the Caribbean a risky proposition. A number of die-hard pirate captains still pursued what they called "the sweet trade" in the West Indies and along the coast of North America. But the more ambitious ones went looking for bigger prizes in that long-time hotbed of piracy, the Indian Ocean. The area was even more attractive to pirates now that merchantmen of the British East India Company were sailing to and from the company's headquarters in Bombay. Even more alluring were the huge, slow-moving galleons of the Great Mogul, the Muslim ruler of India. His ships left India filled with spices and silks, sailed to the Arab ports of Jedda and Mocha, and returned loaded down with gold and silver.

In 1696 a New England customs officer wrote that

the Caribbean pirates "have found out a more profitable and less hazardous voyage to the Red Sea, where they take from the Moors [Muslims] all they have without resistance and bring it to some one of the plantations in the continent of America or islands adjacent, where they are received and harboured and from whence also they fit out their vessels."

Expeditions from North America to the Indian Ocean and back became so common that the route was christened the "Pirate Round." Of all the pirate captains who sailed the eastern seas, the most infamous was Henry Every (sometimes spelled Avery), whose exploits earned him the nickname the Arch-Pirate.

Because so many legends grew up around Every, it's hard to be sure of the facts. Captain Charles Johnson, whose 1724 book *A General History of the Robberies and Murders of the most notorious Pyrates* is one of the main sources of pirate lore, says that Every was born near Plymouth, England—probably about 1653—and was "bred to the Sea."

The Arch-Pirate's seafaring career began innocently enough, first as a sailor in the Royal Navy, then in the merchant marine. At some point he was hired by the governor of Bermuda to transport slaves from Africa. Every was even more unscrupulous than most slavers. He lured Africans aboard his ship under the pretext of trading with them, then seized their gold and sold them as slaves.

Every wasn't physically imposing—he was of medium height and rather chubby—but he was intelligent and self-disciplined. He seldom drank or lost control of his temper, and he was contemptuous of anyone who did. In 1694 he joined the crew of the English privateer *Charles II,* whose commander was, as Johnson puts it, "mightily addicted to Punch." One night, while the captain was in a drunken stupor, Every led the discontented crew in a mutiny. They put the captain ashore, renamed the ship the *Fancy,* and set sail for the Indian Ocean.

In the strait of Bab el Mandeb, at the southern end of the Red Sea, Every lay in wait for the Great Mogul's annual pilgrim fleet, which, after transporting Muslim pilgrims to Mecca, was headed home with a rich cargo. The treasure fleet slipped past the pirates in the night, but the next morning Every ran down two of the slowest galleons. One was the enormous and well-armed *Ganj-i-Sawai,* the grandest vessel in the Mogul's fleet. Its name means "Exceeding Treasure," and it was well named. It carried more than 500,000 pieces of gold and silver— one of the richest single prizes in the history of piracy.

Though the pirates were far outgunned, they got lucky. First one of the *Ganj-i-Sawai*'s cannons exploded accidentally, wreaking havoc on the treasure ship. Then a shot from the *Fancy* splintered the mainmast of the Indian galleon.

Every and his men swarmed aboard. According to a chronicler of the time, the Indian captain was so terrified that he dressed a number of Turkish slave girls in men's clothing and sent them on deck to battle the bandits. More likely the ruse was meant to save the women from being ravished by the pirates. If so, it failed. An East

Henry Every's capture of the treasure-laden Ganj-i-Sawai—pictured here, with Every inexplicably on shore—inspired hundreds of unemployed sailors to try their hand at the "sweet trade."

India Company dispatch reports that the pirates "did do very barbarously by the passengers," including an aged woman relative of the Great Mogul himself. Some avoided the pirates' clutches by jumping overboard or stabbing themselves. Others died from the abuse they suffered.

The haul was so huge that, when it was divided up, each member of the 400-man crew got well over £1,000—twice as much as the average sailor could expect to earn in his whole lifetime. When word of the attack reached India, angry mobs attacked English homes and stoned one of the residents to death. Indian troops surrounded the British East India Company's factory and threw sixty-eight of its officers in prison. The company and the English government offered a combined reward of £1,000 for Every's capture.

Meanwhile Every had sailed west to the Caribbean. With his new-found wealth he tried to buy a pardon from the governor of Jamaica but was informed that pardons could be granted only by the king. Weary of the pirate life, Every decided to return home to England. Unfortunately most of his crew had spent a good deal of their money on liquor. When the *Fancy* was struck by a storm, they were so drunk that they ran the ship aground, damaging it beyond repair.

Every bought two small sloops and, with two dozen of his men, sailed to Ireland. There the pirates split up. But instead of lying low, they were foolish enough to flaunt their wealth and eventually all were arrested—all except Every.

Three Tales of Treasure

Like walking the plank, buried treasure is a phenomenon that occurs far more often in literature than it ever did in life. For the most part, pirates were not the sort to put something aside for a rainy day. Immediately after a prize was plundered, the booty was divided up according to agreement and, as soon as possible after that, spent. Exquemelin writes that, upon reaching port, his fellow *boucaniers*, "according to their custom, wasted in a few days in taverns all they had gained, by giving themselves up to all manner of debauchery. Such of these Pirates are found who will spend two or three thousand pieces of eight [about £500–£750] in one night."

There are a handful of documented cases, though, of pirate captains secreting chests full of coins in out-of-the-way places. The Dutch *boucanier* known as Roche Brasiliano confessed under torture by agents of the Spanish Inquisition that he had hidden over 100,000 pieces of eight on Isla de Pinos, off Cuba. The Spanish promptly claimed it.

Sometime in the early eighteenth century the cruel pirate captain Edward Low buried a chest containing Spanish and Portuguese coins on Isle Haute, near Nova Scotia. According to local legend, the headless ghost of a crewman killed by Low still roams the island. An apparently genuine map of the period led treasure hunter Edward Rowe Snow to search the area with a metal detector in 1952. Snow uncovered a human skull and a handful of gold and silver coins dating back to 1710.

In 1720 two sailors from the merchant ship *Prince Eugene* reported to authorities that their captain had acquired from pirates in Madagascar some £9,000 worth of Spanish silver dollars. The crew, they said, had buried the money in six wooden boxes near the mouth of the York River in Virginia. No one knows whether the treasure was ever recovered.

Stories and paintings that depict pirates burying their treasure generally overlook or conveniently ignore the fact that a chest containing two cubic feet of gold coin would weigh in the neighborhood of two thousand pounds.

Wild rumors about the Arch-Pirate and his exploits were circulating around Britain. One claimed that Every had captured the Mogul's beautiful daughter, married her, and settled down in Madagascar, another that Every had offered to pay off the country's national debt in exchange for a pardon. Popular ballads recounted Every's supposed adventures. Daniel Defoe, the author of *Robinson Crusoe*, wrote a novel, *The Life, Adventures and Piracies of Captain Singleton*, based on Every's career. *The Successful Pirate*, a stage play featuring a hero much like the Arch-Pirate, premiered in 1713.

No one knows for certain what became of Every. According to Captain Johnson, the Arch-Pirate settled in Devonshire, where he arranged with some local merchants to dispose of his loot. But they cheated him badly and, when he complained, threatened to expose him to the authorities. Johnson concludes that "our Merchants were as good Pyrates at Land as he was at Sea."

Three

The Prince of Villains

When news of the riches to be won in the East reached England and America, it started an epidemic of "Red Sea fever." By the late 1690s dozens of pirate ships were cruising the Indian Ocean like sharks searching for prey. The "Red Sea Men" needed a safe haven, a place where they could recuperate, take on supplies, and make repairs.

The large island of Madagascar, off the east coast of Africa, proved to be the perfect pirates' lair. It lay within easy striking distance of the trading routes. Its coastline was pocked with secluded coves. Though England, France, and the Netherlands had all tried to establish colonies there, no European country claimed the island.

But then, in 1699, the English navy began sending warships into the area to combat the surge of piracy. Rather than do battle with such heavily armed vessels, many pirates simply fled. Most of them ended up back in the Caribbean. In 1716 the governor of Virginia wrote that "A nest of pirates are endeavouring to establish themselves in New Providence and . . . may prove dangerous to the British commerce, if not timely suppressed."

He was right. New Providence Island in the Bahamas

Captain Misson's Mission

One of the pirate captains profiled in *A General History of the Pyrates* is a mysterious Frenchman known only as Captain Misson. According to Captain Johnson, while Misson was serving aboard a privateer, the *Victoire,* he fell in with a lapsed Catholic priest named Caraccioli, who convinced him and many of the crew that organized religion and organized government were corrupt and oppressive. Caraccioli's philosophy was that "every Man was born free, and had as much Right to what would support him, as to the Air he respired."

When the officers of the *Victoire* were killed in battle, the crew elected Mission their new captain and "resolved with him upon a Life of Liberty." At first this liberty consisted of raiding Turkish, English, and Dutch ships. But Misson did not want to be like the general run of pirates, "who are Men of dissolute Lives and no Principles." He would not allow cursing or drinking on board the *Victoire*. He treated captured sailors with unusual kindness and generosity, and freed any slaves he found.

Misson's goal was to establish a "retreat," a colony where men could live in racial and economic equality. He found the ideal site for his retreat on the island of Madagascar. He and his men made friends with the local people; some, including Misson and Caraccioli, even married Malagasy women, and for a time, they lived the sort of life Misson had envisioned.

But then a band of English pirates arrived, and the utopia, which Misson called Libertalia, began to unravel. The two factions quarreled, and it became clear that the colony needed some form of government and a set of laws. Misson was elected Lord Conservator for a period of three years.

He served very little of his term because, without warning and seemingly without reason, the Malagasys turned against the colonists, killing some and driving the rest out. Shortly afterward, Misson died when his ship foundered in a storm. But some of his men survived, and one of them, says Captain Johnson, passed on to him a manuscript telling the story of Captain Misson.

Though Johnson's account is thorough and full of convincing detail, scholars are generally agreed that neither Misson nor his colony ever existed. Probably the myth of Libertalia was just an idealized expression of the desire for freedom and equality that lured so many men into a life of piracy.

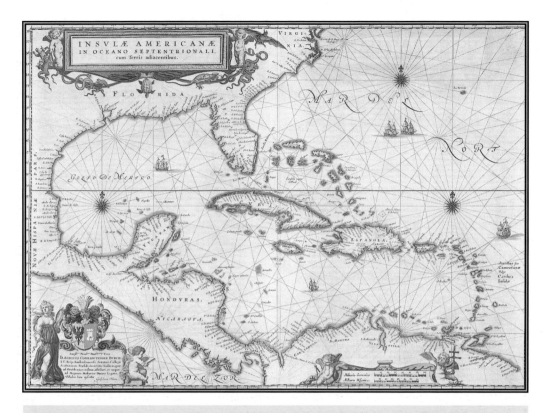

Though this 1660s Dutch map (with Latin inscriptions) of the Caribbean makes no mention of New Providence Island, forty years later the island was so notorious for its wild lifestyle that pirates, it was said, dreamed of going not to heaven but to New Providence.

swiftly replaced Madagascar as the pirates' paradise. Next to the harbor a filthy, lawless tent city known as Nassau sprang up. From here a whole new generation of marauders sailed forth to savage ships throughout the West Indies and up and down the coast of America. The governor of Jamaica complained that "There is hardly one ship or vessel coming in or going out of this island that is not plundered."

Irate English merchants convinced the Crown to

appoint Woodes Rogers, a former privateer, governor-in-chief of the Bahamas. When Rogers arrived in Nassau in July 1718, there were roughly a thousand pirates in residence. The new governor offered each of them a full pardon and a plot of land, and most accepted.

But a stubborn few continued their criminal ways. One of these was Edward Teach who, under the alias Blackbeard, became perhaps the most notorious pirate of all time—a rather astounding accomplishment, considering his career as an outlaw lasted barely two years.

Historians disagree about where and when Blackbeard was born. According to Captain Johnson, Teach hailed from Bristol, home to more pirates and privateers than any other English port. He was born around 1690, and started his seafaring career aboard a privateer during the War of the Spanish Succession. When the war ended, Teach, like many other sailors, was out of a job. He drifted to New Providence Island, where he joined a pirate band.

By 1717 Teach had proven himself so courageous and capable that he was given a ship of his own, a captured French vessel that he renamed *Queen Anne's Revenge.* His first big prize was an English merchant ship, which he looted and burned. When the Royal Navy station in Barbados learned of the attack, it sent the *Scarborough,* a frigate armed with thirty guns, in pursuit of Teach. Instead of fleeing, Teach decided to fight and damaged the *Scarborough* so badly that it backed off.

This daring victory made Teach's name famous throughout the Caribbean. Shrewd self-promoter that he was, he capitalized on it. Knowing that a pirate's best weapon was a fearsome image, he set about creating one for himself. His appearance was striking to begin with; one sailor described him as "a tall, spare [lean] man with a very black beard which he wore very long"—the source, obviously, of his nickname, Blackbeard.

To make himself look more terrifying, Teach dressed all in black and plaited his unruly beard into braids tied up with black ribbons. Before each battle he stuck pieces of hemp called gunner's matches under the brim of his hat and lit them, wreathing his head in smoke. Captain Johnson writes that these features, plus his "fierce and wild" eyes, "made him altogether such a Figure, that Imagination cannot form an Idea of a Fury, from Hell, to look more frightful."

Teach also cultivated a reputation for being temperamental and unpredictable. He did this so successfully that some of his own crew considered him insane, or possessed by the Devil. Captain Johnson relates how Teach once challenged several of his men to "make a Hell of [our] own, and try how long we can bear it." They shut themselves up in the hold of the ship with pots of burning sulfur. His companions soon burst out, gasping for air. Blackbeard emerged, then, "not a little pleased that he held out the longest," and cried, "The next time we shall play at gallows and see who can swing longest on the string without being throttled."

Sometimes his whims were positively cruel. One night, as he and his navigator sat drinking together, Teach suddenly blew out the candle, drew a pair of

Blackbeard's wild appearance was calculated to strike fear in the hearts of his foes. Note the smoking gunner's matches protruding from under his hat.

pistols, and fired them off under the table. One shot wounded the navigator in the knee, crippling him for life. When the crew demanded the reason for this, Teach replied that "if he did not now and then kill one of them, they would forget who he was."

Now that Nassau was being civilized by Governor Rogers, Teach made the secluded inlets and coves along the North Carolina coast his base of operations. Though most of the colonies were now discouraging pirates, North Carolina's economy was so depressed that its governor actually welcomed them—provided they gave him a share of their profits. Blackbeard's favorite refuge was the area around Ocracoke Inlet; a cove there is still known as "Teach's hole."

In May 1718 Teach made the most audacious raid of his career. He anchored at the mouth of Charleston harbor in South Carolina and seized the cargo of every ship that came by. Aboard one of these ships was a member of the governor's council and his four-year-old son. Teach announced that he was holding them hostage, demanding as ransom a sizable stock of medicines— probably those needed to treat syphilis, a venereal disease that was widespread among the free-living pirates. If the ransom wasn't paid within two days, Teach said, all anyone would see of the hostages was their heads.

Because of bad weather the medicines weren't delivered until after the deadline. Unpredictable as always, Teach spared the hostages' lives, but kept their clothing, sending them ashore in their underwear.

Teach now had half a dozen vessels of various sizes

Between attacks on ships trading among the colonies, pirates holed up in the many secluded coves along the coast of the Carolinas and caroused at local taverns.

and a total crew of over three hundred. In such a large company, there were bound to be some who spoke out against their captain. As usual Teach chose an unorthodox method of dealing with the situation. He ran the

Queen Anne's Revenge aground, loaded all the loot and supplies aboard another ship, the *Adventure,* and, with a small, handpicked crew sailed away, leaving the rest to fend for themselves.

Back in the safety of North Carolina's coves, Blackbeard took a wife, a sixteen-year-old girl. One writer of the time commented that "this, I have been informed, made Teach's fourteenth wife, whereof a dozen might still be living." This was probably just another of the many legends that grew up around Blackbeard. He may well have been at least a bigamist, though, for the governor of Jamaica reported that "This Teach it's said has a wife and children in London."

Not all the citizens of North Carolina were as tolerant as their governor. When word got around that Blackbeard meant to establish a pirate kingdom there, some locals appealed for help to Governor Alexander Spotswood of Virginia. Spotswood had a long-standing hatred of Teach, whom he called the "Prince of Villains." In November 1718 the Virginia governor chartered two sloops, the *Ranger* and the *Jane,* manned them with sailors from two Royal Navy warships, and dispatched them to Ocracoke Inlet.

When Teach saw the ships approaching, he seemed unconcerned; probably he didn't think they could navigate the shallow waters of the inlet. Instead of preparing for battle, he and his men spent the night carousing.

By the following day the two sloops were within shouting distance. "At our first salutation," reported Lieutenant Robert Maynard, who commanded the *Jane,*

While the Virginia legislature debated whether to approve funding for an expedition to chase down Blackbeard, the impatient governor, Alexander Spotswood, put up the money himself, including a reward of £100, for the pirate's capture.

"he drank Damnation to me and my Men, whom he stil'd [styled] Cowardly Puppies, saying, He would neither give nor take Quarter."

The pirates fired a load of small shot, nails, and scraps of iron that wounded or killed many of the *Ranger's* crew. A second volley raked the *Jane.* Maynard sent his men belowdecks, to fool Teach into thinking that the ship was defenseless. When the pirates swung aboard the *Jane,* the English sailors sprang upon them. Maynard fired his pistol point blank at Blackbeard, but the bullet seemed not even to faze the pirate captain. He attacked with his cutlass so fiercely that he broke Maynard's sword in two. Before Blackbeard could strike again, one of Maynard's men delivered a thrust to his throat.

Yet Teach fought on. According to Maynard's account, the pirate took another nineteen sword wounds and four more bullets before he finally collapsed. Maynard had Blackbeard's head cut off and his body thrown overboard. Legend has it that the corpse swam in circles for some time, searching for its head, which was suspended from the bowsprit of the *Jane* as a grisly trophy.

Some say Blackbeard's skull later turned up, coated with silver, at the University of Virginia, where fraternity pledges were obliged to drink wine from it as part of their initiation rites.

Four
Two Willful Women

The Caribbean pirates became more cautious after Woodes Rogers executed eight of their number at Nassau in December 1718. When England went to war with Spain yet again in 1719, many pirates accepted a pardon from the British king, George I, and did their plundering under the title of privateer.

One of those who came to New Providence to accept the Acts of Grace, as the pardon was called, was a flamboyant, small-time pirate, John Rackam, nick-named Calico Jack after the colorful trousers he wore. Jack might never have resumed his outlaw career had it not been for an unexpected development: he fell in love.

The object of his affection was a willful young woman of nineteen, Anne Bonny. In a statement she made at her trial for piracy, Anne revealed that she was the daughter of a prominent Irish lawyer, William Cormac. Her mother was the Cormacs' household maid. Though Cormac dressed Anne as a boy and passed her off as his apprentice, eventually the truth came out, and such a scandal ensued that Cormac decided to make a new start in the New World.

He and the maid and Anne settled in Charleston,

Though he looks fairly fearsome in this woodcut, Calico Jack was cut from very different cloth than the likes of Blackbeard and L'Olonnois. He attacked mostly small, defenseless vessels and had no stomach for torture or murder.

South Carolina. Anne displayed her feisty nature early on. One possibly exaggerated account has her attacking a servant girl with a knife in a fit of anger. When a young man made unwelcome advances toward her, says Captain Johnson, "she beat him so, that he lay ill of it a considerable Time."

No doubt she felt stifled by the staid community of Charleston, so much so that when a ne'er-do-well sailor named James Bonny asked her to marry him and elope to New Providence Island, she accepted. There the dashing Calico Jack caught her eye, and vice versa.

Jack was so smitten that he offered to buy Anne from her husband. Indignant, Bonny complained to the governor, who threatened to have Anne flogged if she was unfaithful. Anne and Jack promptly hatched a plan to run away together. Along with some of Rackam's old mates, they boarded the *William,* a merchant sloop in Nassau harbor, and took command of it.

Since women were not welcome aboard pirate vessels—they were thought to bring bad luck—Anne disguised herself as a man. For six months or so the *William* cruised the Caribbean, looting mostly small merchant ships and fishing vessels. When the pirates took a large Dutch merchantman, Rackam coerced some of its sailors into joining his crew.

Anne, who was clearly not a one-man woman, was strongly attracted to one of the new recruits, a blond, blue-eyed English sailor. She made her feelings known, only to discover that the sailor was, in fact, a twenty-seven-year-old woman named Mary Read.

Later, when Mary was on trial, she, too, recounted her early life. Like Anne, she was born out of wedlock. Mary's mother had recently lost another young child, a boy; to keep Mary's birth a secret, her mother dressed her in the dead child's clothing. When she reached her teens, Mary, still disguised as a boy, enlisted in the British cavalry. She somehow managed to keep her sex a secret —until she fell in love with the man who shared her tent. The two troopers married and mustered out, then opened a tavern in Holland.

When her husband died of a fever, Mary resumed her masquerade, first as an infantryman, then as a sailor on the Dutch ship that fell prey to Calico Jack. As Anne had done, Mary concealed her femaleness for some time. But then romance reared its head again, in the form of a good-looking fellow named Tom Deane, who had joined the pirates against his will.

Tom, who apparently wasn't much of a fighter, crossed one of Jack's men and was challenged to a duel. Fearing for her sweetheart's life, Mary provoked the same man into dueling with her. Thanks to her years of soldiering, she was an accomplished swordswoman, and she skewered her opponent—undoubtedly saving Tom from a similar fate.

After that Mary abandoned her disguise, and Anne followed suit. A member of the crew recalled that "when

Four More Feisty Females

Anne Bonny and Mary Read were not the first women, by any means, to be seduced by the sweet trade—nor would they be the last. According to the Danish historian Saxo Grammaticus, Alwilda (or Alvilda), the daughter of a fifth-century Scandinavian king, fleeing from an arranged marriage, fell in with a band of pirates and proved herself so capable that they elected her their captain. Under her leadership, the pirates ravaged the Baltic Sea, forcing the king of Denmark to send armed ships after them, commanded by none other than Prince Alf, Alwilda's intended husband. Alf's skill and daring in battle so impressed Alwilda that she consented to marry him after all.

During the reign of Queen Elizabeth I, Irishwoman Grace O'Malley became famous for "her stoutness of courage and person, and for sundry exploits done by her at sea." From her base at Rockfleet Castle on Ireland's west coat, she plundered passing merchant ships until the local governor dispatched a force that seized her fleet of some twenty vessels and imprisoned one of her sons. Grace made the long trip to London to plead in person with the queen. As a result, the governor set her son free.

In 1773 Fanny Campbell, an eighteen-year-old Massachusetts girl, watched her fiancé, William Lovell, sail away on a voyage from which he never returned. Two years later, the faithful Fanny learned that William had been captured by pirates and was now wasting away in a Havana prison, accused of piracy himself. Disguised as a man, Fanny

they saw any vessel, gave chase, or attacked, they wore men's clothes; and at other times they wore women's clothes." When the pirates boarded a prize, the two fought alongside the men, every bit as fiercely. A lady on board one of the unlucky vessels reported that they "wore mens jackets, and long trousers, and handkerchiefs tied about their heads; and that each of them had a machet [sword] and pistol in their hands, and cursed and swore."

signed aboard a trading vessel, took command of it, and sailed it to Cuba, where she masterminded the release of her fiancé and ten other American prisoners.

When Chinese pirate-king Cheng I died in 1807, his wife, Cheng I Sao—or Mrs. Cheng—took his place and, for the next three years, headed up an outlaw fleet that eventually included over two hundred large ships, at least six hundred smaller ones, and some seventeen thousand pirates! Every government force sent to capture Mrs. Cheng and her followers was defeated. But when the Chinese enlisted the help of the British and Portuguese navies, Mrs. Cheng wisely decided to accept the government's offer of a pardon. She went on to run a popular gambling house and died peacefully in 1844 at the age of sixty-nine.

Fanny Campbell's pirate crew went on to become privateers during the American Revolution. Fanny married her sweetheart, William Lovell, and never went to sea again.

So far Calico Jack and company had been lucky in avoiding the pirate-chasing privateers enlisted by Woodes Rogers. When their luck ran out, it wasn't due to the presence of women on board, but to their own carelessness.

In October 1720 the pirates anchored at the western tip of Jamaica and began drinking and carousing, unaware that cruising nearby was a heavily armed privateer sloop. When they were discovered, the crew

If Mary Read had actually sported the sort of neckline shown in this eighteenth-century engraving, it's highly unlikely she could have posed as a man so successfully.

of the *William* tried to flee, but the ship was disabled by a shot from the privateers, who came alongside and climbed aboard. Jack and his men hid belowdecks, leaving only Mary and Anne to defend the ship. Furious, Mary opened a hatch and fired both her pistols into the midst of her cowardly mates, killing one and wounding another.

Though the women fought like wildcats, they were overpowered, and the pirates were taken in chains to stand trial. Most were sentenced to hang. Tom Deane, Mary's lover, convinced the judge that he had been forced to join the crew and escaped the noose.

There was a strong prejudice among sailors against the presence of women on a ship. But Anne Bonny and Mary Read proved that, in a fight, they were more valuable than any of the male crew members.

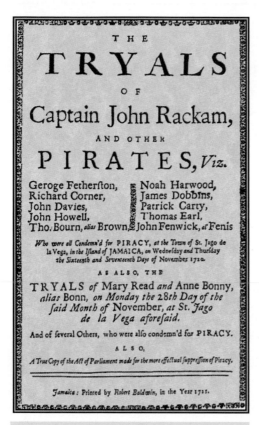

THE
TRYALS
OF
Captain John Rackam,
AND OTHER
PIRATES, *Viz.*

Geroge Fetherſton,   Noah Harwood,
Richard Corner,   James Dobbins,
John Davies,   Patrick Carty,
John Howell,   Thomas Earl,
Tho. Bourn, *alias* Brown, John Fenwick, *at* Fenis

Who were all Condemn'd for PIRACY, *at the Town of St. Jago de
la Vega, in the Iſland of* JAMAICA, *on Wednesday and Thurſday
the Sixteenth and Seventeenth Days of November* 1720.

AS ALSO, THE
TRYALS *of* Mary Read *and* Anne Bonny,
alias Bonn, *on Monday the 28th Day of the
ſaid Month of* November, *at St. Jago
de la Vega aforeſaid.*

And of ſeveral Others, who were alſo condemn'd for PIRACY.

ALSO,

A True Copy of the Act of Parliament made for the more effectual ſuppreſſion of Piracy.

Jamaica: Printed by *Robert Baldwin,* in the Year 1721.

In writing about the women
pirates, Captain Johnson admits
that "some may be tempted to
think the whole story no better
than a novel or romance." But
evidence such as this account of
the trial makes it clear that their
tale is true.

Mary and Anne were tried separately and were also condemned to death. When the judge asked if they had anything to say in their defense, they replied, "Milord, we plead our bellies." Both women were pregnant, and since English law prohibited the killing of an unborn child, they were imprisoned instead.

On his way to the gallows Calico Jack was allowed to see Anne one last time. She was less than sympathetic. She was, she said, "sorry to see him there, but if he had fought like a Man, he need not have been hang'd like a Dog."

Mary Read contracted a fever in her prison cell and died, in April 1721, before her baby could be born. Anne's fate is uncertain, but according to some accounts, friends of her father bought her freedom, and she and her child returned home to South Carolina.

Five

The King of Ranter Bay

With the heat on in the New World, pirate captains began drifting back to Africa in search of big prizes. The Red Sea route again became a target, and Madagascar regained some of its former glory as an outlaw outpost. For some pirates, it was more than just a temporary haven; it was a place to retire to. A man with a little ill-gotten gold could lead a life of ease there, surrounded by liquor, good food, and friendly women—provided, of course, he survived the gamut of tropical diseases.

The most enterprising and influential former pirate ever to settle there was James Plantain, the self-styled King of Ranter Bay. Plantain was born in Jamaica, to English parents. He went to sea at the age of thirteen; by the time he was twenty, he had turned pirate. According to his own account, he only took up the sweet trade to raise the capital he needed for an honest career.

He did, in fact, use the proceeds from several seasons of looting Indian treasure ships to set himself up in business, though it was not a notably honest one. In 1720, the year of Calico Jack's capture, Plantain and two partners settled at Ranter Bay (now called Antogil Bay), a harbor on the northeast coast of Madagascar, and built a sumptuous castlelike mansion protected by a stockade

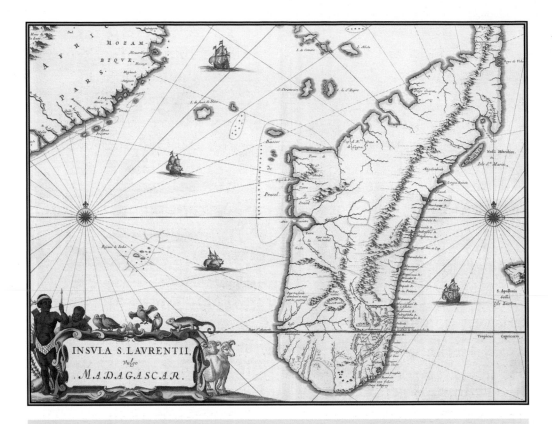

INSVLA S.LAVRENTII, vulgo MADAGASCAR.

The fourth largest island in the world, Madagascar provided plenty of room for pirate enclaves. Ranter Bay, the site of James Plantain's little kingdom, is the deep indentation at the northeast corner of the island.

armed with cannon. This fort became the trading and social center for the area, and Plantain became the most powerful man in northern Madagascar. Though he was still only in his early twenties, Plantain's strong will and air of self-assurance made him a natural leader. These same qualities, unfortunately, led him into trouble.

According to a sailor who visited Ranter Bay, Plantain "had many [Malagasy] wives whom he kept in great subjection, and after the English manner called them Moll, Kate, Sue, and Peg . . . They were dressed in the richest silks and some of them had diamond necklaces." But King James wanted a more suitable queen. He settled on a young beauty named Eleanora Brown, whose father was an English pirate and whose mother was the daughter of a local chieftain called King Dick. Because she could recite the Lord's Prayer and the Ten Commandments, the girl was known as Holy Eleanora.

King Dick apparently didn't consider Plantain worthy of his granddaughter, for he refused to give her up. Furious, Plaintain declared war on Dick. Plantain won the decisive battle and Eleanora's hand, but soon discovered that Eleanora was not quite as holy as he'd imagined. In fact she was pregnant by one of King Dick's pirate allies, who had been killed in the fighting. Plantain blamed King Dick for Eleanora's condition and had the chieftain put to death. But he treated Eleanora herself like royalty, bringing in twenty household slaves to wait on her.

Now that he had his queen, the King of Ranter Bay set out to make himself monarch of the whole island. His main opposition was another Malagasy chieftain who had established a settlement on the site of the failed French colony of Fort Dauphin, at the southern end of the island. After an eighteen-month siege the chieftain surrendered, and Plantain proclaimed himself king of Madagascar.

The new despot didn't rule wisely. He set himself up as a slave trader; anyone who opposed or displeased him was sold to one of the slave ships that called at the

Pirate captains were expected to prove their right to rule by fighting it out hand to hand with anyone who challenged them. When James Plantain's authority was questioned, he preferred to resign.

island. When his subjects began to protest and plot against him, King James decided it was time to give up his crown. He had a sloop built especially for him, loaded it with loot, put Eleanora and their children aboard, and sailed away from his pirate kingdom.

Just where the deposed king sailed is uncertain. One legend says that he ended his days peacefully somewhere in India. Despite Plantain's faults, under his rule Madagascar had prospered. After he departed, conditions on the island rapidly went downhill. Within a decade there was no trace left of the pirates' paradise that had once flourished there.

Six

Black Bart

The east coast of Africa wasn't the only part of the continent to attract outlaws. By the early 1700s European trading posts dealing in gold, ivory, and slaves had sprung up along the west coast, around the Gulf of Guinea. This area, called the Guinea Coast, became a favorite hunting ground for pirates, including Bartholomew Roberts. Nicknamed Black Bart, Roberts was probably the most reckless, daring, and atypical pirate of the so-called Golden Age. He was also the most successful by far; in his three-year criminal career he captured an astounding total of four hundred ships.

Roberts, who was born in Wales around 1682, had no particular interest in following the sweet trade. His great ambition was to be a captain in the Royal Navy. But after twenty years as a seaman aboard navy and merchant vessels, he began to realize that, because he came from a working-class family and not from the nobility, the Admiralty probably would never make him an officer, let alone give him command of a ship.

In 1719 Roberts was third mate on the *Princess*, a slave trader operating along the Guinea Coast. The *Princess* was captured by the pirate captain Howell Davis, and many of its merchant seamen were forced to join

Though most pirate captains preferred small ships and a relatively small crew, Black Bart's flagship—pictured here in the foreground—was enormous, with fifty cannons and a crew of over two hundred.

the crew of Davis's ship, the *Royal Rover*.

At first Bartholomew Roberts was reluctant to turn outlaw. He simply wasn't the type. He was dignified and disciplined, and he dressed impeccably. Because of his strict religious upbringing, he frowned on those two favorite pirate pastimes, gambling and drinking; his beverage of choice was tea. He was, furthermore, thirty-six years old; by that age, most pirates were either retired or dead.

His air of superiority must have impressed the crew of the *Royal Rover*. When Captain Davis was killed in an ambush, they turned to Roberts for leadership. It was an offer he couldn't refuse. Though the ship wasn't exactly the sort he'd dreamed of commanding, it was likely to be his only chance at a captaincy, and he took it. "It is better to be a commander than a common man," he said, "since I have dipped my hands in muddy water and must be a pirate."

He found the life of an outlaw more appealing to him than the one he had known on merchant and navy ships. "In an honest service there is thin rations, low wages and hard labor; in this, plenty and satiety, pleasure and ease, liberty and power. . . . No, a merry life and a short one shall be my motto."

Roberts was a demanding captain. He drew up a list of strict regulations that every crew member was obliged to agree to. If anyone objected, he was invited to dispute the matter with Roberts, using a pistol and sword. But Black Bart was also fair. He seldom forced captured sailors to turn pirate unless they had some special skill. These men were offered an "insurance policy" stating that they had joined against their will.

Roberts and his loyal followers devised a different sort of policy to insure that they would never be tried and hanged. "If we are captured," said one crewman, "we will set fire to the powder with a pistol, and all go merrily to Hell together."

Under Roberts's influence the pirates became relatively civilized—or at least played at it. They called one another Your Lordship and referred to themselves as the House of Lords. But when it came to plundering, they were no gentlemen.

They attacked ships along the Guinea Coast for a time, then decided to try their luck off the Portuguese colony of Brazil. After robbing a merchant ship of £50,000 in gold coins, they sailed into the Caribbean but were chased off by privateers and Royal Navy ships. They continued north to Newfoundland, where they captured a whole fleet of unsuspecting traders and fishing boats without firing a shot. Roberts's raid was so audacious that the governor of New England wrote, "One cannot withhold admiration for his bravery and daring."

But Black Bart's daring had a reckless quality to it. It was almost as though he was determined to make certain his life was, as his motto declared, a short one. In September 1720 he deliberately returned to the Caribbean, now a notoriously unhealthy place for pirates, and boldly set about looting every merchantman he encountered.

Despite his civilized manner, Roberts could be ruthless in his treatment of captured sailors, especially those who hailed from Martinique and Barbados, islands whose governors had been unrelenting in their efforts to capture him. According to one report, "Some they almost whipped to death, others had their ears cut off, others they fixed to the yard arms and fired at them as a mark." Black Bart's pirate flag featured a likeness of himself standing atop two skulls, one labeled ABH (A Barbadian's Head), the other AMH (A Martinician's Head).

Black Bart's pirate flag

By the spring of 1721 Roberts had singlehand-edly brought shipping in the West Indies to a virtual halt. With a short-age of ships to prey on, the House of Lords voted to return to their old haunts in the Gulf of Guinea. Undeterred by the fact that two British men-of-war were now patrolling the coast, the pirates proceeded to plunder ships anchored at the slaving port of Whydah.

The commander of the HMS *Swallow* set off in pursuit of Roberts and caught up with him at Cape Lopez. The pirate crew, hung over from a hard night's drinking, barely managed to raise their sails. Then, to their dismay, instead of fleeing, Roberts impudently and inexplicably ordered them to sail straight for the British ship.

The Royal Navy cannoneers opened fire, shattering one of the pirate vessel's masts. A burst of grapeshot struck Roberts in the throat. Seeing their bold captain dead, many of the hardened pirates burst into tears. As Black Bart had always requested, they threw his body into the ocean. With him went all their will to fight. Instead of blowing up the ship and themselves, as they had once vowed to do, the House of Lords simply surrendered.

In this picture, the British man-of-war HMS Swallow *displays her true colors. As it approached Roberts' ship, though, it was flying a French flag. Roberts and his men didn't realize they were in danger until one of the pirates, a deserter from the British navy who had once sailed on the* Swallow, *recognized his old ship.*

The English authorities at Cape Coast Castle in Africa dealt severely with Roberts's crew. Seventeen were imprisoned; another twenty were sentenced to hard labor in the mines on Africa's Gold Coast; fifty-two were hanged. The bodies of eighteen were dipped in tar, bound with iron hoops, and hung from gibbets atop the nearby hills as a warning to other would-be pirates.

Seven

The Patriotic Pirate

The execution of Roberts's men was just the latest in a series of strict measures aimed at wiping out piracy. The previous year, the British Parliament had passed a piracy act declaring that anyone who traded with pirates or even sold supplies to them would be considered an outlaw, too. In addition, crews of merchant ships who fought off pirate attacks were to be rewarded, and those who failed to resist would be punished. For the first time, honest seamen had a compelling reason to stay honest. The sweet trade had gone sour. Though there were still isolated acts of piracy, the age of rich prizes and pirate kingdoms was over.

Well, almost.

About a hundred years later, piracy in the Caribbean enjoyed a whole new heyday, more abbreviated than the first, but nearly as golden. The cast of characters in this second act were not quite as memorable, but the era did produce one of the best known and most intriguing outlaw leaders of all time—Jean Lafitte.

Though Lafitte lived a century later than Blackbeard or L'Olonnois, facts about his life and exploits are often just as elusive, thanks to Lafitte's penchant for spreading misinformation about himself. There's even doubt about

Whether Jean Lafitte actually was the son of French aristocrats, as he sometimes claimed, his dress, speech, and manners were those of a cultured gentleman.

the spelling of his name; the pirate himself usually signed it *Laffite*.

In 1837, only sixteen years after Lafitte's career

ended, a volume titled *The Pirates' Own Book* appeared. The author, Charles Ellms, claimed to have drawn on original documents and eyewitness accounts. According to him, Lafitte was born in France in 1781 and spent several years plundering ships in the Indian Ocean. But many historians now believe that Lafitte was actually born in Haiti and that his looting was confined to the Caribbean.

Tall and slim, with elegant manners, Lafitte cut quite a romantic figure. Legend says that he married a rich, beautiful woman who fell ill when she and Jean were marooned on a barren island by Spanish soliders. When she died soon after, Lafitte declared all Spaniards his enemies.

In 1808 Lafitte established a headquarters on Grand Terre Island, at the mouth of Barataria Bay, about sixty miles due south of New Orleans. Within a year the base had attracted thousands of outlaws and misfits from all over the West Indies. When Spanish colonies in Central and South America began a general revolt, Lafitte obtained letters of marque from the newly formed Republic of Cartagena (now part of Colombia) that authorized him to attack Spanish vessels.

But Lafitte considered ships of all nations, including the United States, fair game. His usual strategy, after capturing a prize, was to kill the entire crew, change the name of the vessel, and sell its cargo in New Orleans. Often the cargo consisted of slaves, even though the United States had banned the importation of slaves in 1807.

When some of these slaves incited a bloody rebellion, Louisiana's governor William C. C. Claiborne decided it was time to crack down on Lafitte and offered a $500 reward for the pirate's arrest. The defiant Lafitte offered in turn a reward of $5,000 to anyone who would bring Claiborne to him.

At the outbreak of the War of 1812, the British began making plans to control the crucial port of New Orleans. They offered Lafitte a commission in the Royal Navy and a healthy bonus of $30,000 if he would fight on the side of the Crown. If he declined they would destroy Barataria, as the pirates called their island stronghold.

By the early 1800s, New Orleans was a major trading center—and a major center for smuggling activity.

The Rewards of Not Resisting

If the crew of a captured vessel surrendered without a fight, they could usually expect to be treated reasonably well. But sailors who were foolish enough to resist a pirate attack risked suffering a wide variety of ingenious and inhuman punishments. The pirates were not just taking their revenge; they were establishing a precedent, so the crew of the next prize they encountered would think twice about fighting back.

Several penalties were so popular—not with their victims, of course —that they acquired special names. *Sweating* involved stripping the prisoner naked and chasing him around the mainmast, prodding him with sharp tools and weapons—humiliating, but not necessarily fatal. *Woolding* was worse. As Exquemelin describes it, the victims "had slender cords or [gunner's] matches twisted about their heads, till their eyes burst out of the skull."

Being marooned, or abandoned on a desert island, was a slower way to die, but usually just as sure. A pirate crew often meted out this punishment to their own mates who had committed some offense such as stealing from a fellow pirate or deserting during battle.

Oddly, the form of retribution that most of us associate with piracy, walking the plank, seems to have been extremely rare. One of the few recorded incidents took place in 1822, long after the end of the Golden Age, when the captain of the Jamaican sloop *Blessing*, unable or unwilling to produce money on demand, was forced to take a long walk off a short plank laid across the rail of his own ship.

Lafitte stalled the British and offered his services to Governor Claiborne instead, at no cost. All he asked was a pardon for him and his men. "I am the stray sheep wishing to return to the fold," he wrote.

Claiborne responded by ordering the army and navy to launch an attack on Barataria. Claiborne's men captured eighty of the outlaws, half a million dollars' worth of goods, and sixteen ships. Lafitte himself escaped, but according to one story, during the raid his new bride,

The rarely used practice of making a victim walk the plank must have seemed like a relatively benign fate compared with some of the tortures that pirates inflicted on their prisoners.

a girl of only fourteen, was killed by a stray shot.

Surprisingly, Lafitte remained loyal to the American cause. When General Andrew Jackson arrived in New Orleans in December 1814, the pirate offered to provide him with arms and manpower. Though Jackson was reluctant to join forces with outlaws, his army was so small that he had little choice.

After the American victory at the Battle of New Orleans, President James Madison pardoncd the pirates, noting that they "have manifested a sincere penitence . . . that they have exhibited, in the defense of New Orleans, unequivocal traits of courage and fidelity."

When the war ended there was another surge of crime in the Caribbean, as thousands of former privateers, suddenly thrown out of work, turned pirate. Jean Lafitte was among them. Though he couldn't convince the government to return his ships, he managed to buy back eight of them and sailed west to desolate Galveston Island to establish what he called "an asylum to the armed vessels of the party of independence"—in other words, a pirate kingdom.

Lafitte built a mansion that he called Maison Rouge, after its red-painted walls, and armed it with cannon. Like Barataria, and like New Providence and Madagascar before it, the island attracted, in the words of a New Orleans customs officer, a "motley mixture of freebooters and smugglers."

The kingdom flourished for a year. Then, in the fall of 1818, a hurricane swept the island, drowning thousands of the inhabitants, leveling Maison Rouge, and sinking fourteen pirate vessels. Though Lafitte's men rebuilt their "asylum," it never quite regained its prominence. When an American navy warship arrived in Galveston in 1821 with orders to evacuate the pirates, Lafitte, now described as "a stout, rather gentlemanly personage," gave up the island without a fight, even obligingly putting his town to the torch.

As uncertain as his origins are, even less is known about Lafitte's ultimate fate. Ellms claims that the pirate went on raiding in the Caribbean and was killed during an attack on a British ship. Other sources offer other possibilities: he died of a fever on Mexico's Yucatán Peninsula; he ended up in Illinois, where he met Abraham Lincoln; he began a new life in Charleston, South Carolina, under the alias John Lafflin.

Piracy in the Caribbean didn't die out with the fall of Jean Lafitte, but it was on its last sealegs. The ship that evicted Lafitte from Galveston was part of a navy fleet that was now patrolling the Gulf Coast and the West Indies. By 1826 one of the officers was able to report that "Depredations on our commerce are fortunately unheard of where they were formerly so frequent." The short-lived second golden age of piracy had come to an end.

GLOSSARY

Alexander the Great (356–323 B.C.)   King of Macedonia whose vast empire once stretched from Greece to India.

Arawak   An Indian people who occupied northern South America and the islands of the Greater Antilles (Cuba, Jamaica, Hispaniola, Puerto Rico) before the Spanish conquest of the sixteenth century.

British East India Company   A trading company chartered by Queen Elizabeth I in 1600 to break the Netherlands's monopoly on the Eastern spice trade. At the height of its power, the company was authorized to coin money, enforce the law, and even declare war.

cutlass   A heavy sword with a thick, slightly curved blade.

Elizabeth I (1533–1603)   Queen of England from 1558 to 1603.

frigate   A large but swift three-masted ship with square sails.

galleon   A four-masted warship or merchant vessel with triangular sails on the two rear masts.

gallows   A wooden frame consisting of two uprights and a cross beam from which condemned criminals were hanged.

Galveston Island   An island on the Gulf coast of Texas. In the early nineteenth century, Galvez-town, as it was called, belonged to Mexico.

gibbet   A frame similar to a gallows, but with a projecting arm, generally used for displaying the corpse of an executed criminal.

grapeshot   A cluster of small iron balls fired from a cannon.

gunner's match   A fuselike cord made of hemp fibers. When lighted, it burns at a slow rate and is used to set off the gunpowder in a cannon or musket.

Hispaniola   The second largest island in the West Indies (after Cuba), now divided into the nations of Haiti and the Dominican Republic.

indentured servant   A worker who is bound by a contract to serve a specified number of years. In exchange, the employer usually agrees to pay for the worker's passage on a ship.

letters of marque and reprisal   Official documents issued to a ship's captain authorizing him to seize the cargo of vessels of an enemy nation.

Madagascar   An island the size of Texas that lies about 250 miles off the southeast coast of Africa. The indigenous people, the Malagasy, are mainly Malaysian and Polynesian in origin.

man-of-war   A heavily armed frigate that carries a large crew of fighting men.

pieces of eight   Old Spanish silver coins worth eight reals apiece.

Polo, Marco (about 1254–1324)   A Venetian merchant and explorer who, at the age of seventeen, began a long journey through central Asia and China.

privateer   A sailor or ship licensed by a particular nation to attack that nation's enemies.

Ptolemy   Second-century Greek astronomer and geographer who developed the theory that the sun and planets revolve around the Earth.

Red Sea   A long, narrow body of water that divides northeast Africa from the Arabian Peninsula. The strait of Bab el Mandeb at the southern end connects the Red Sea with the Indian Ocean.

Saxo Grammaticus (about 1150–1220)   Danish historian and poet, author of *Historica Danica*, a sixteen-volume history of the Danes.

sloop   A single-masted ship that is faster and more maneuverable than a frigate or galleon and can sail in shallower water.

Spanish Inquisition   A religious and political body created by the Spanish king and the pope to seek out and punish heretics.

utopia   A land or country that boasts an ideal social, political, and economic system, such as the imaginary island of the same name in Sir Thomas More's 1516 book, *Utopia*.

War of the Spanish Succession   A thirteen-year conflict (1701–1714) that pitted Spain and France against the Grand Alliance, which included Britain, Austria, and Hungary.

TO LEARN MORE ABOUT PIRATES

Books—*Nonfiction*

DePauw, Linda Grant. *Seafaring Women*. Boston: Houghton Mifflin, 1982.
 This well-written, well-researched book by a professor of American history
 tells of women mariners from the twelfth-century pirate princess Alvilda
 to the first woman commander of a Coast Guard cutter.

Garwood, Val. *The World of the Pirate*. New York: Peter Bedrick, 1997.
 Heavily illustrated look at the history and lifestyle of pirates worldwide,
 written by an officer of the English National Maritime Museum.

Kallen, Stuart A. *Life among the Pirates*. San Diego: Lucent, 1999.
 Part of Lucent's The Way People Live series. A thorough, accurate, well-
 written overview of pirate life during the Golden Age, with lots of quotes
 from original sources.

Platt, Richard. *Pirate*. New York: Knopf, 1994.
 One of the popular Eyewitness series. A sketchy history of piracy from
 Ancient Greece to the 1850s, light on text but heavy on illustrations—
 period pictures, paintings, photos of artifacts.

Shuter, Jane, ed. *Exquemelin and the Pirates of the Caribbean*. Austin, TX:
 Steck-Vaughn, 1995.
 Part of the History Eyewitness series. A simplified and greatly abridged
 version of Exquemelin's *Pirates of the Caribbean*, with illustrations and
 brief explanatory passages on each page.

Wilbur, C. Keith. *Picture Book of the Revolution's Privateers*. Harrisburg, PA:
 Stackpole, 1973.
 Not the usual sort of picture book, but an unusual close-up look at various
 aspects of shipboard life in the eighteenth century, illustrated with detailed
 line drawings. A treasure trove of offbeat information, from how to furl a
 sail to how to make hardtack to how to board an enemy ship.

Books—*Fiction*

Yolen, Jane. *The Ballad of the Pirate Queens*. New York: Harcourt Brace, 1995.
 A lively picture book for all ages. Yolen's rollicking verses tell a fanciful
 version of the careers of Anne Bonny and Mary Read.

On-line Information*

http://www.sonic.net/~press/
 Provides links to dozens of sites about Caribbean pirates.

http://www.piratesinfo.com
 Divides its information into two categories—Fact and Legend. Each has a

number of rather skimpy subcategories, such as history, famous pirates, pirate ships, pirate vocabulary.

http://www.buccaneer.net/
Offers pirate books, maps, and other artifacts for sale.

Video

Pirates: Passion & Plunder. Vol. 2—Pirates of the New World. Chicago: Questar Video, 1995.

A combination of documentary and dramatization, this film, which was shown on the Discovery Channel, is often melodramatic and sometimes amateurish, but entertaining.

Historic Sites

Jean Lafitte National Historical Park and Preserve. Park Headquarters, 365 Canal Street, Suite 3080, New Orleans, LA 70130-1142 (504) 589-3882.

A network of parks that includes Barataria and the site of the Battle of New Orleans.

Web sites change from time to time. For additional on-line information, check with the media specialist at your local library.

BIBLIOGRAPHY

Botting, Douglas, and the editors of Time-Life Books. *The Pirates.* Alexandria, VA: Time-Life, 1978.

Carse, Robert. *The Age of Piracy.* New York: Grosset & Dunlap, 1965.

Cordingly, David. *Under the Black Flag: The Romance and the Reality of Life among the Pirates.* New York: Random House, 1995.

Cordingly, David, ed. *Pirates: Terror on the High Seas—from the Caribbean to the South China Sea.* Atlanta: Turner, 1996.

Defoe, Daniel. *A General History of the Pyrates.* Columbia, SC: University of South Carolina Press, 1972. [At the time this edition was published, Defoe was generally believed to be the real author.]

Ellms, Charles. *The Pirates.* New York: Gramercy, 1996. [A new edition of *The Pirates' Own Book.*]

Esquemeling, John. *The Buccaneers of America.* London: George Allen & Unwin, 1951. [When Alexander Exquemelin's book was translated into English, the publishers altered his name to John Esquemeling.]

Haring, C. H. *The Buccaneers in the West Indies in the XVII Century.* Hamden, CT: Archon Books, 1966.

Jameson, J. Franklin, ed. *Privateering and Piracy in the Colonial Period:*

Illustrative Documents. New York: Augustus M. Kelley, 1970.

Mitchell, David. *Pirates.* New York: Dial, 1976.

Nesmith, Robert I. *Dig for Pirate Treasure.* New York: Devin-Adair, 1958.

Rankin, Hugh F. *The Golden Age of Piracy.* New York: Holt, Rinehart and Winston, 1969.

Remini, Robert V. *The Battle of New Orleans.* New York: Viking, 1999.

Ritchie, Robert C. *Captain Kidd and the War against the Pirates.* Cambridge, MA: Harvard University Press, 1986.

Sherry, Frank. *Raiders and Rebels: The Golden Age of Piracy.* New York: Hearst, 1986.

Snow, Edward Rowe. *True Tales of Pirates and Their Gold.* New York: Dodd, Mead, 1953.

Wheeler, Richard. *In Pirate Waters.* New York: Crowell, 1969.

Whipple, A. B. C. *Pirate: Rascals of the Spanish Main.* New York, Doubleday, 1957.

NOTES ON QUOTES

The quotations in this book are from the following sources:

Introduction

Page 8, "the most intense": Sherry, *Raiders and Rebels: The Golden Age of Piracy,* p. 7.

Page 10, "Jesus bless us!": Esquemeling [Exquemelin], *The Buccaneers of America,* p. 55.

Page 10, "the conduct of all privateers": Botting, *The Pirates,* p. 25.

Chapter One: The Bloodthirsty Buccaneer

Page 13, "took several handfuls": *The Buccaneers of America,* p. 80.

Page 13, "I shall never": *The Buccaneers of America,* p. 82.

Page 15, "would instantly cut them": *The Buccaneers of America,* p. 103.

Page 15, "like a ravenous wolf": *The Buccaneers of America,* p. 104.

Page 15, "history of the life": *The Buccaneers of America,* p. 117.

Chapter Two: The Arch-Pirate

Page 18, "have found out": Mitchell, *Pirates,* p. 102.

Page 18, "bred to the Sea": Defoe, *A General History of the Pyrates,* p. 50.

Page 19, "mightly addicted": *A General History of the Pyrates,* p. 51.

Page 21, "did do very barbarously": *Pirates,* p. 106.
Page 22, "according to their custom": *The Buccaneers of America,* p. 72.
Page 24, "our Merchants were as good": *A General History of the Pyrates,* p. 57.

Chapter Three: The Prince of Villains
Page 25, "A nest of pirates": Botting, *The Pirates,* p. 137.
Page 26, "every Man was born": *A General History of the Pyrates,* p. 389.
Page 26, "resolved with him": *A General History of the Pyrates,* p. 391.
Page 26, "who are Men": *A General History of the Pyrates,* p. 393.
Page 27, "There is hardly": Botting, *The Pirates,* p. 138.
Page 29, "a tall, spare man": Cordingly, *Under the Black Flag: The Romance and the Reality of Life Among the Pirates,* p. 13.
Page 29, "fierce and wild" and "made him altogether": *A General History of the Pyrates,* p. 85.
Page 29, "make a Hell": *A General History of the Pyrates,* p. 85.
Page 29, "not a little": *A General History of the Pyrates,* p. 85.
Page 29, "The next time": Botting, *The Pirates,* p. 148.
Page 31, "if he did not": *A General History of the Pyrates,* p. 84.
Page 33, "this, I have been": Rankin, *The Golden Age of Piracy,* p. 114.
Page 33, "This Teach": *Under the Black Flag,* p. 71.
Page 35, "At our first salutation": *Under the Black Flag,* p. 196.

Chapter Four: Two Willful Women
Page 38, "she beat him so": *A General History of the Pyrates,* p. 164.
Page 39, "when they saw": *Under the Black Flag,* p. 64.
Page 40, "her stoutness of courage": *Under the Black Flag,* p. 72.
Page 40, "wore mens jackets": *Under the Black Flag,* p. 64.
Page 44, "Milord, we plead": *Raiders and Rebels,* p. 276.
Page 44, "sorry to see him": *A General History of the Pyrates,* p. 165.

Chapter Five: The King of Ranter Bay
Page 46, "had many wives": *Pirates,* p. 192.

Chapter Six: Black Bart
Page 52, "It is better": Botting, *The Pirates,* p. 161.
Page 52, "In an honest service": Botting, *The Pirates,* p. 31.
Page 52, "If we are captured": *Raiders and Rebels,* p. 331.
Page 53, "One cannot withhold": Botting, *The Pirates,* p. 165.
Page 53, "Some they almost whipped": *Under the Black Flag,* p. 130.

Chapter Seven: The Patriotic Pirate

Page 60, "had slender cords": *Under the Black Flag,* p. 131.

Page 60, "I am the stray": Ellms, *The Pirates,* p. 42.

Page 61, "have manifested": Ellms, *The Pirates,* p. 44.

Page 62, "an asylum": Wheeler, *In Pirate Waters,* p. 78.

Page 62, "a motley mixture": Snow, *True Tales of Pirates and Their Gold,* p. 20.

Page 62, "a stout, rather gentlemanly personage": *In Pirate Waters,* p. 97.

Page 63, "Depredations on our commerce": *In Pirate Waters,* p. 171.

INDEX

Page numbers for illustrations are in boldface